A Portrait of GIBSONS

By Vene Parnell

Below the treed shoulder of Mt Elphinstone, the village of Gibsons lies nestled in the rising mists of dawn on the protected shores of Howe Sound. A fishing boat departs the harbour, gently rippling the calm water, a silent silhouette plying an ageless tradition. A tall blue heron stands intently fishing in the stillness, as a soaring bald eagle glides high above a passing flight of Canada Geese.

The early rays of morning sun brighten the waters of Howe Sound in glowing pinks and golds, painting the contrast of the forested slopes on Keats Island and beyond them, the dramatic peaks of the Coast Mountain range, rising steeply above the tide.

It is nature's timeless gentle awakening kiss.

From the time of the arrival of the first natives to the BC coast some 2,000 years ago, the peaceful splendour of this wilderness setting still dominates the life and rhythms of tiny Gibsons, a scenic town of 4,000 people, curved around a natural harbour.

Although it is only 15 km from the expanding city of Vancouver, Gibsons is a safe haven that seems light-years removed from the noise and bustle of big-city life. Gibsons keeps its distance via a ferry crossing of Howe Sound, a natural barrier of steep mountains and islands that preserves its rural west coast feeling. From the earliest days, Gibsons has attracted summer visitors from Vancouver to this swimming, fishing and cottage playground. For over 100 years, it has been known for its gentle climate as the "gateway" to the Sunshine Coast.

Above left: Dramatic colours of sunrise are reflected in the calm morning waters of Howe Sound. (also previous page).

Top: The delicate lily-like wild-flower, Brodiaea, is found on the coast's rocky shorelines.

Left: Autumn mists settle over Gibsons harbour.

Above: Mussells thrive in the fast currents of Gibsons "Gap," providing food for starfish and seagulls.

Right: A great blue heron rests on a piling in Gibsons Harbour. On the left can be seen Armour's Beach and Soames Hill look-out known as "the Knob."

With homes perched on rocky bluffs along the sea, and surrounded by creeks tumbling into treed ravines, the rich bounty of forests and fish continues to sustain the life of Gibsons. Amid the 400 berth marina and the busy government wharf, salmon still return here to spawn, geese and ducks raise their young, and otter and seals swim and feed. A wealth of mussells, clams and star-fish thrive in the strong tidal movements around the Gibsons "Gap," which forms the narrow rocky entrance into the harbour from Georgia Strait.

Named for its founder, George Gibson, it is easy to imagine the strong attraction the town's pioneer settler must have felt when he first gazed upon the dramatic beauty of Howe Sound. Since that time, the splendour of this scenery has exerted its magic and become familiar to millions of people around the world through the immensely popular Canadian TV show *The Beachcombers*.

Filmed in Gibsons, against the rugged coastal backdrop of scenic islands and snow-capped mountains, the show has been seen in over 35 countries since 1970, attracting thousands of visitors each year to the famous old café of Molly's Reach at the head of Gibsons wharf.

Close by in Pioneer Park, a bronze replica of George Gibson stands on the site of his first homestead, gazing over the harbour view from his final resting place.

Gibsons harbour entrance is protected by a gazebo and a breakwater promenade. The new log-built office of the Gibsons Harbour Authority overlooks the town wharf.

In the image of its first independent resident, Gibsons wears the mantle of fame with a somewhat stoic and bemused air. The daily routines of small-town life continue undisturbed for the hardworking loggers, fishermen and real-life beachcombers who move stray logs along the shoreline. Dinghies and crab traps sit in front of seaside homes and cottages, while children swim from pilings and floats under the watchful gaze of cormorants, herons and seagulls.

Tugs and work-boats tow logs and barges to log-sorting grounds in Howe Sound and to nearby Port Mellon, where BC's oldest operating pulp mill is the coast's largest employer. The fishing fleet brings in shrimp and prawns, salmon, black cod, crab and halibut and brisk sales of fresh seafood attract both residents and visitors to the Gibsons Dock beside Molly's Reach. Sea kayaks and racing outrigger canoes enter in and out of the Harbour gliding past sail-boats and all sizes of pleasure craft. And all this activity takes place in the majestic lee of the Coast Mountain range, rising 2100 metres above the rugged scattering of islands of Howe Sound, one of the world's most beautiful natural settings.

Above: A great blue heron rests in the early morning sun and watches over the harbour.

Far right: A commemorative statue of George Gibson stands in Pioneer Park, overlooking the harbour and Molly's Reach.

MARINA
BOAT LAUNCH
LIBRARY
SHOPS
POST OFFICE
ACCOMMODATIONS
MUSEUM

Molly's
Reach

Gibsons' natural history goes back over 5 million years, when tall and stately 1261 m (4,000 ft) Mt Elphinstone was formed along with nearby Keats, Gambier and Bowen Islands. Thousands of years ago, as glaciers retreated up Howe Sound, they gouged the rocky headlands of Gibsons Bluff and Gospel Rock, depositing gravel, sand and glacial till where the flat harbour and townsite of Gibsons sits today. It is believed the narrow and shallow Shoal Channel entrance into Gibsons harbour, between Gibsons and Keats Island, is a remnant of this glacier activity. The popular beaches of the town were also formed: Pebbles, Franklin and Georgia Beach on the Georgia Strait side along with Armour's Beach and nearby Grantham's, Soames and Hopkins beaches facing into Howe Sound.

The thick spruce, fir and cedar forests and the native Indian inhabitants that followed the melting glaciers lived here undisturbed until the 1791 and 1792 explorations of British Captain George Vancouver and his Spanish counterparts Captains Galiano and Valdes, all of whom left maps of this area.

Above: Tall mossy trees and lush ferns grow along a rainforest trail on the Sunshine Coast.

Right: The showy "fairy-tale" mushroom, Amanita Muscaria, is poisonous, but many edible varieties of mushrooms thrive on the coast.

For his contributions, Vancouver's name has lived on in the city of Vancouver and Vancouver Island. He named Jervis Inlet, Howe Sound, Burrard Inlet, Point Atkinson and two of the islands in this vicinity, Anvil and Passage Island. The Strait of Georgia was named in honour of King George III. His greatest local contribution was the name of Gower Point, which showed on Vancouver's chart at the "Gap" entrance into Howe Sound and Gibsons Harbour, now known as Dougall Point. It is believed Captain Vancouver was the coast's first European visitor, as it has been recorded that his ship, the *Discovery*, stopped here to replenish fresh water supplies for his voyage.

It was a Captain Richards on the survey vessel *Plumper* in 1859 and 1860 who finished the naming of many of the local islands, including his ship's namesake, Plumper Cove, a popular marine park on Keats Island, located just a mile away from Gibsons. Bowen, Gambier, Keats, Hutt and Pasley Islands were all named by him in honour of British Admiralty officers.

Mount Elphinstone's lofty name honours an old Scottish peerage whose first member, William Elphinstone was Lord High Chancellor of Scotland in 1488 and who founded the University of Aberdeen in 1494. At the time of Captain Vancouver's explorations, the 11th Lord Elphinstone was the First Lord of the British Admiralty.

A full moon casts a magic glow over Howe Sound.

A cairn commemorating Captain Vancouver's historic visit to these shores sits near Chaster Creek on the Ocean Beach Esplanade. Here Chaster Park marks the end of Gibsons' long, meandering street known as Gower Point Rd. It is possible that the first white man to set eyes on Mount Elphinstone may have been a much earlier explorer, Juan de Fuca. Exploring north from Mexico he claimed that in 1592 he sailed into the Strait of Georgia through an opening from the Pacific Ocean that today still bears his name.

Other area names derived from the families who followed George Gibson to this coast: Grantham's Landing, Soames Point and the 253 m (800 ft) high Soames Hill view-point known locally as the "Knob", Hopkins Landing, Williamson's Landing and Dougall Point. Chaster Creek was named for the founder of a popular summer resort of the 1920's and 30's known as Bonniebrook, where spawning salmon can be observed in the fall beside the elegantly restored Bonniebrook Lodge Bed & Breakfast. The western boundary of Gibsons is Payne Rd, where in the early days of logging in the 1880's, a skid road was built from Payne Creek to bring logs downhill to the site of Gibsons present day wharf.

Above: Gower Point Road follows the Georgia Strait shoreline from Gibsons to Bonniebrook Beach.

Opposite: The cairn marking Capt George Vancouver's historic landing in 1792 sits near Chaster Creek, facing west towards Vancouver Island.

Hard-working Finnish settlers arrived on the coast in 1905. They cleared land and originated a community with a store and a Post Office on the flat land above the harbour known as Gibsons Heights, where the shopping malls and many of Gibsons businesses stand today. Some of these families were disillusioned immigrants escaping the coal mines of Vancouver Island and others were from the experimental Utopian commune of Sointula on Malcolm Island. The Finnish people brought with them a love of agriculture and independent political ideals, strong influences that are still felt in Gibsons to this day.

In 1906, a fire destroyed everything for 8 kms to the west of the new settlement of Gibsons, and although most homes were saved, for the first time in its recorded history, the forested land was completely bare. This encouraged agricultural development and for over 20 years a berry cannery produced strawberry jam. It became Gibsons first commercial enterprise that was not directly derived from the area's rich forest and fish resources. Small organic markets and sheep farms still operate along Reed and Henry Roads, on the outskirts of the town, selling wool, jams and fresh produce to supplement the gardens of local residents.

Opposite: Brilliant colours of sumac glow in autumn sunlight.

Below left and right: The mild coastal winters allow grapes, bamboo, palms and banana trees to flourish in Gibsons gardens.

Above: A fresh snowfall is a rare but beautiful sight on the Sunshine Coast.

Apple trees still blossom and grow on an old homestead along North Road.

West of Bonniebrook on the Strait of Georgia lies a one mile stretch of south facing waterfront owned by the Boy Scouts, known as Camp Byng. Beyond the camp is Robert's Creek, a woodsy coastal community established by Thomas Roberts in 1890 at the mouth of the creek where his family built a dock and a store. Today's "Creek" residents are mainly gardeners, artists and retirees who are devoted to preserving the trees of the rainforest as well as a gentler rural pace of life. Roberts Creek's beautiful beaches, sunny climate and mellow lifestyle were the inspiration for the name "Sunshine Coast," bestowed by the Roberts family over 100 years ago to attract city visitors to this area.

The curve of Bonniebrook beach faces west towards Roberts Creek on the Strait of Georgia.

Right: The colorful 50 foot mandala, painted by 300 local residents along the shoreline of Roberts Creek, is a vibrant display of the artistic energy of the "Creekers."

Below right: The folksy Gumboot Cafe in the heart of Roberts Creek is a popular stop for healthy meals, art and music events.

The native Indians who came to these shores both revered and adapted to the wealth of the woods and wildlife by establishing villages and using the giant cedars for canoes, clothing and building materials. The very first contacts with Europeans were built on the fur trade, and there were plentiful otter, bear, beaver, wolves, cougar and mountain goats in the steep inlets of Jervis and Sechelt and along Howe Sound. The Hudson's Bay Company established trading posts in the early 1800's at Nanaimo, Fort Langley

and Victoria. Later, coal-mining on Vancouver Island and forestry on the coast generally became the primary industries of the new "wilderness" land, named by Queen Victoria in 1858 as British Columbia.

~

Although generically, the name Coast Salish includes a large number of coastal tribes, the Sechelt (Shi-shalh) Indians a few miles upcoast from Gibsons were a different group from the Squamish (Sko-mish) Indians who had a village site known as Chek-welp where the town of Gibsons now stands. In his book, "The Gibsons Landing Story," local author, teacher and historian, Lester Peterson, claimed that a large shell midden below the soil in the vicinity of Armour's Beach indicates an aboriginal occupation of about 2,000 years. The Indians lived here alongside the first white settlers until 1892, when smallpox caused them to abandon their village and the site was then used only sporadically for hunting and fishing until 1925. A line of summer homes leased on the Chek-welp reserve land now extends along the beach from Gibsons town boundary as far as Granthams Landing.

The terrible decimation of the Indian tribes by smallpox severely reduced the coastal native populations. The reserve treaties of the 1870's gave rights to the Squamish Indians at their old village site of Chek-welp and at the mouth of Soames Creek, as well as a small bay near the Port Mellon pulp mill, and the tiny Shelter Islands near Plumper's Cove.

Opposite, far left: The twisted red peeling bark is distinctive of arbutus trees, found growing on rocky shorelines.

Opposite, right: A grave marker by the old site of a Squamish Indian village stood for many years near the mouth of the Rainy River at Port Mellon.

Below: A sunset over Vancouver Island is viewed from the Gospel Rock look-out in Gibsons.

The next dramatic impact on the Indians and rainforests of the Sunshine Coast came in the great surge of logging in the 1870's. Wood was needed to build the busy new settlements of New Westminster, Vancouver, Victoria and Nanaimo. The wealth of firs, spruce and cedars were the prime targets of this activity. The immense girths of these majestic trees, recorded in old photographs, have left behind their silent evidence in the huge stumps still visible under today's second growth forests. Many of Gibsons' streets are based on the old skid roads that were built by the early loggers to bring their logs down to the water. Today, Howe Sound is a major booming and sorting ground for westcoast logs.

For all practical purposes, the Gibsons and Sechelt areas were selectively logged of the biggest and most

Steam rises into the night air from Howe Sound Pulp and Paper at Port Mellon, the oldest active pulp mill in British Columbia. Built in 1908, the mill is the coast's largest employer. A major modernization project in 1988 included the installation of state of the art paper-making machines in partnership with Oji Paper of Japan, along with major improvements to meet environmental emissions standards.

accessible trees before the homesteaders arrived in the 1880s. Logging continued with the arrival of the early settlers who made a living cutting cedar shingle bolts and wood for fueling the steam-ships and tugs that were the life-line to the new coastal settlements. Around the turn of the century, with the innovation of pulp mills, the plentiful hemlock and alder trees were also taken, to feed the world's growing demand for paper.

Above: A self-loading log barge is towed into Howe Sound by a sturdy tug.

Left: The protected waters of Howe Sound near Gambier Island are ideal for log booming grounds and are used to sort a majority of BC's westcoast timber.

W hen George William Gibson arrived here in May of 1886, at the age of 57, he was a retired lieutenant of the Royal Navy. Born January 31, 1829 at Lincolnshire, England, George went to sea at the early age of 12, and after his seafaring days he emigrated to Ontario where he spent many years as a market gardener. He also lived in Michigan for a time and once won first prize at the Chicago World's Fair for growing the largest rhubarb. He married August Charlotte Purdy at Bay City, Michigan, and the Gibsons had two sons, George and Ralph, and 6 daughters.

In 1885, the Gibson family came to Vancouver Island, via San Francisco. George hand-built a 30 foot boat near Nanaimo and sailed off with his sons searching for land for his family.

The story is told how George's small boat, the *Swamp Angel* weathered a storm one night at Keats Island. In the morning the men sailed through the gap entrance into Howe Sound and discovered the protection of Gibsons' natural harbour. George, who wanted to support his family by gardening and fishing, must have felt he had discovered the safety of a beautiful paradise. There were fresh artesian springs in the rich silted soil, eel grass growing in the shallow waters of the bay supported herring, cod and salmon, and with his small boat he could transport his fish and produce and sell it in the city of Vancouver.

Opposite top: A flower bedecked house boat is an attraction in Gibsons' busy harbour.

Opposite bottom: George Gibsons' statue stands in Pioneer Park in front of the landmark heritage home of the coast's first doctor, Dr. Frederick Inglis.

Right: A view of Gibsons from the top of Soames Hill, known locally as the "Knob." Vancouver Island can be seen 32 kms in the distance across the Strait of Georgia.

Above: Gibsons 400 berth marina is a popular weekend destination for Vancouver boaters

Right: Gibsons Yacht Club and Marina boasts a flower garden on the Seawalk.

Opposite top: A summer evening stroll on the breakwater boardwalk is a pleasant way to enjoy the harbour sights. Mount Elphinstone is in the background.

Opposite bottom: A cedar salmon carving welcomes boaters to Gibsons.

George and his sons wasted no time in each pre-empting 65 hectares, land that was free for the taking from the Crown through a scheme to lure settlers to the "wild wastes" of Canada's new western colony. Ralph pre-empted nearby Pasley Island and George, along with his other son George, Jr., claimed District Lots 686 and 685, the basis of today's townsite of Gibsons. However, in order to have money to build a home, the Gibson men fished and also worked in the construction boom in Vancouver. There is an historic photograph taken in June, 1886, of Vancouver's Mayor and Council seated in front of a tent marked City Hall after the big fire that burned that city to the ground. George can be seen in the background, standing on Vancouver's new City Wharf, which he was helping to build at that time. He most likely had no inkling that he himself would soon become the unofficial mayor of another new settlement that would one day bear his name.

Shortly after, in 1887, the Gibsons' oldest daughter, Mary, and her husband George Glassford arrived to settle on DL 687, next to George's property. They had travelled west from Ontario on one of the first cross-country CPR trains to Vancouver and their daughter, Grace, who later married into the pioneer Chamberlin family, was the first white child to be born in Howe Sound.

In 1888, George Soames pre-empted the next waterfront section, DL 694 and in 1890, Chuck Winegarden, who married Emma, another Gibson daughter, claimed a section just north of Hopkins Landing. Next door to them, near today's Langdale ferry terminal, was land claimed by Dr. Alex Forbes, medical officer to the Squamish Indians and discoverer of both the copper mine of Brittania Beach in Howe Sound and the iron deposits on Texada Island. Other settlers quickly followed and in 1890, the first school was opened with 10 boys and 13 girls. It has been recorded that the first teacher's salary was $50 monthly.

Below: A mural by artist Ben Owens, at Gibsons' waterfront Winegarden Park, features a traditional killer whale motif by Squamish artist Siobhan Joseph.

Right: Two historic landmarks stand at Gibsons wharf—Smitty's Marina and Molly's Reach on the street directly above.

Right: A view of Gibsons Harbour attracts hundreds of visitors to famous Molly's Reach.

Below: A bronze sculpture of George Gibson stands among heritage roses in Pioneer Park, beside the graves of Gibson family members. It was created by artist Jack Harman who also designed the famous equestrian statue of Queen Elizabeth II at the Parliament Buildings in Ottawa.

As the settlement grew, George Gibson built the first wharf and a store where Molly's Reach now stands, and became Gibsons first postmaster, magistrate, and harbourmaster. This store burned in 1910 and the present Molly's Reach was built in 1930 by Charles Percival Smith, who bought the Gibson property. Eventually this family established Smitty's Marina on the boardwalk below the wharf, another well-known feature of the Gibsons waterfront. Molly's Reach has served as a candy store, a hardware store and a liquor store. It has also been a grocery store, a second-hand store, a real estate office and achieved world fame in 1971 when it became the set of a make-believe cafe for "The Beachcombers" CBC-TV show for 19 years. The upstairs was used for make-up, wardrobe and dressing rooms for the stars of the show.

Today's Molly's Reach is a busy cafe where meals are served to visitors who come to see the "Home of the Beachcombers" from countries as far away as Australia, Japan, Germany, Greece and South America, as well as Canada's own Arctic Circle. The story of "The Beachcombers" can still be seen in re-runs and portrays the small-town atmosphere of Gibsons, the drama of men and the sea, of loggers and salvagers and cafes that serve hearty, man-sized meals. It is Canada's longest running TV drama and celebrated its 30 years of fame by filming a special 2 hour TV show in Gibsons called "The New Beachcombers" in 2002. The town of Gibsons has also "starred" in other shows such as the Stephen King movie "Needful Things", filmed here in 1992, and recently, in 2003, in a TV series "Colombo" episode.

Pioneer George Gibson, third from right, built the first store at the head of the wharf in 1900. Mrs. Gibson stands beside him and his two daughters, Hattie (Mrs. Albert McColl, far left) and Nellie, beside her husband Don Patterson, are in this photo. The store burned in 1910 and today's Molly's Reach was rebuilt on the site in 1930 by the Smith family, owners of Smitty's Marina.

City of Vancouver Archives:
OUT P708N312

At the turn of the century, in 1900, a LePage factory was built in the harbour to manufacture glue from dog-fish livers, but it operated only briefly. These fish continued to be in demand for the valuable oils from their livers until after World War II. The great Fraser River sockeye salmon runs brought about the busy salmon fishery with canneries built along the coast as far north as Rivers Inlet and the Nass and Skeena Rivers. The plentiful salmon provided food and a livelihood for most of the early coast settlers and still attract hundreds of sports fishermen to Gibsons and the Sunshine Coast.

Gibsons' protected harbour is home to a commercial fishing fleet of over 20 boats who go as far north as the Queen Charlotte Islands to fish for salmon, black cod, shrimp, prawns, krill, tuna and halibut. The harbour bustles with the constant activity of a large assortment of trollers, tugs, barges, water taxis, beachcombing boats as well as sailboats and visiting pleasure boats.

Above: Gibsons active fishing fleet brings in catches of salmon, black cod, halibut, crab and prawns and fresh seafood is sold in the harbour.

Opposite far left: Maple leaves glow in the setting sun.

Opposite near left: Cedar carvings of salmon by local artist Steve Stevens, form a dramatic entrance to the new log Harbour Authority building on Gibsons wharf, shown at right.

When Dr Frederick Inglis, the Coast's first doctor arrived in 1912, he built the landmark heritage home overlooking the harbour which served as a surgery as well as a residence for his family. His son, Dr. Hugh Inglis continued the medical practise and lived in this distinctive home until the 1960's.

Gibsons most famous politician, James S. Woodsworth, and his family stayed for a time at the Inglis home while he served here as a Methodist minister in the last years of World War I. He became a Member of Parliament and founder and first national leader of the Co-operative Commonwealth Federation (CCF) Party, forerunner of Canada's New Democratic (NDP) Party. Independent political thought is still a feature of Gibsons today, with groups representing such diverse interests as the Marijuana Party and the Green Party. As well, there is avid grass roots community involvement in projects such as the waterfront beautification which produced the award-winning breakwater gazebo, promenade and new log home of the Harbour Authority at Gibsons wharf.

Gibsons modern library shares Holland Park with Gibsons Town Hall, Elphinstone Maritime and Pioneer Museum and flocks of Canada Geese. In 1947, the original name of Gibsons Landing was changed officially to Gibsons.

Left: Masses of blooms on a local houseboat are a feature attraction in Gibsons Harbour.

Below: Historic Inglis House, built in 1912, overlooks Pioneer Park and the harbour.

Bottom: Gibsons Heritage Theatre features hand-carved cedar entrance doors by Heiltsuk native artist, Bradley Hunt. The restored building at the corner of North and School Roads began life in 1932 as the Women's Institute Hall.

A stroll along Gibsons historic waterfront is a floral delight, from the beautiful gardens on the seawalk at Gibsons Marina, to the fragrant heritage roses in Pioneer Park, with an abundance of flowering shrubs beside homes and gardens along the way. The coast's mild winters give way to the gentle rains of spring with a burst of colour: camelias, rhododendrons, azaleas, magnolias and lilacs. Brilliant forsythia, miles of yellow broom, and blossoming cherry and apple trees fill the road-sides along with pink and purple fox-gloves, lupines and butterfly bushes. The treed ravines produce shows of bright yellow skunk cabbage, blue-bells, and trillium among the lush undergrowth of ferns, salal, mushrooms, blackberries and salmonberries.

Above: Scented lavender grows in local gardens.

Right: Every spring, pink, white and purple foxgloves brighten local roadsides.

Left: Finding your way around town—the fragrance of heritage roses fills Pioneer Park.

Below: The graceful stems of lupines thrive in woods and gardens.

Bottom: Showy rhododendrons and other blossoming shrubs burst into brilliant colour in spring.

Left: The pretty 20 m cascade of Langdale Falls is a refreshing treat for hikers.

Above: The lush forest undergrowth produces fern fiddleheads in spring.

Opposite, clockwise from top left:
Low-lying Western Trillium blooms in early spring.

The blossoms of dogwood trees, British Columbia's official flower, brighten coastal forests, sometimes blooming twice a year.

Butterfly bush is a plentiful, colorful shrub that grows very quickly in the coastal climate.

Showy yellow skunk cabbage thrives in the moisture of creeks and ravines. Its large leaves were used by the Coast Salish people for steaming food.

From the earliest days, the coast has been serviced by all manner of vessels. Today the BC Ferries is the main transportation link for goods, services and people living on the Sunshine Coast. For tourists enroute to Gibsons, the ferries also provide a spectacular 40 minute sightseeing cruise among the dramatic Coast Mountains and islands of Howe Sound.

Gibsons isolation in its splendid watery setting has created a marine history that lives on in the Maritime section of the Elphinstone Pioneer Museum situated in the heart of Gibsons.In the 1870's coal or wood-burning tug-boats were used to transport loggers and equipment from New Westminster and Vancouver to logging camps on the coast. Later, gravel used for cement and for roads was taken from the beaches and towed to the cities.

Tugs brought the belongings of the early settlers and, they still tow log booms and barges in and out of Howe Sound. Gibsons revives the spirit of its maritime past by hosting old and restored visiting tugs during annual events such as Canada Day and the Sea Cavalcade Festival. Every July, the town celebrates with a week-end of fireworks, dances, a parade, salmon BBQ, swimming and fishing competitions. The highlight is the logger sports, where hard-working men compete to display their logging and booming skills to delighted audiences.

The change from water to land transportation came in 1911 when the first road was built to the "resorts" of Selma Park and Sechelt. Until the road was extended in 1934 to the fishing community of Pender Harbour, boats of the Union Steamships and the Columbia

Mission boat, which served as a hospital, were the life-lines to the coast's early settlements. Gibsons' first truck was a Model T, bought by storeowner Harry Winn in 1912 to deliver lumber and supplies to local customers. Seaplanes have also been a vital passenger link to Gibsons, and they fly in and out of the harbour regularly.

Opposite: Logger sports are a part of the Sea Cavalcade Festival in July and entertain audiences with boom boats, log races, and power sawing contests.

Right: Gibsons busy harbour is full of all sizes of tugs, trollers, houseboats and work-boats.

Below: Stately and elegant Marina House on Gibsons seawalk welcomes visitors to Bed & Breakfast.

Left: BC Ferries Queen of Esquimalt

Below: Langdale, 5 km from Gibsons, is the BC Ferries terminal for the Howe Sound crossing from Horseshoe Bay in West Vancouver to the Sunshine Coast.

Opposite right: Skookumchuk tidal rapids at Egmont is an "extreme sports" destination for white-water kayakers

Opposite far right: The ice-capped fiord of Princess Louisa Inlet, with 36m high Chatterbox Falls, is a world-renowned cruising destination in Jervis Inlet on the Sunshine Coast.

The Union Steamships Company began a coastal service in 1891 and brought passengers, freight and mail across Howe Sound to George Gibson's wharf . This continued until 1951, when the Black Ball Ferries started a 48 car ferry run between Horseshoe Bay and Gibsons. A few years earlier, in 1946, starting with a small cabin cruiser called the *Commuter*, a local company known as the Sea Bus Lines began ferrying passengers between Gibsons and Horseshoe Bay, beginning the growing trend of hundreds of commuters who now ride the ferries to work in Vancouver every morning.

By 1954, the service was expanded to a 60 car ferry and in 1956 two vessels made 14 ferry runs a day. In 1958, a terminal was built at the mouth of Langdale Creek and this greatly relieved the traffic congestion at the busy government wharf . In 1961, the government of BC purchased the Black Ball Ferries in order to operate the "highway link" across Howe Sound from Horseshoe Bay to the Sunshine Coast.

One of the first steamships to call at George Gibson's wharf was the S. S. *Capilano*, built in 1891 and wrecked at Savary Island in 1915. In 1919, it was replaced by a larger *Capilano* which saw over 20 years of service to Gibsons before it became part of the breakwater at Lund, at the opposite end of the Sunshine Coast. The well-known MV *Lady Rose*, still operating in Barkley Sound on Vancouver Island, began its coastal service in 1937, crossing Howe Sound to Gibsons until 1951.

Today the 50 mile "Sunshine" coastline is a popular holiday vacationland that ends at another ferry crossing to Powell River, over the steep fiord of Jervis Inlet. This is the access to the boating destinations of Malibu Resort, the waterfalls of Princess Louisa Inlet, and the highly dramatic Skookumchuk tidal rapids at Egmont, at the entrance to Sechelt Inlet. The coastal road, Highway 101, winds from Gibsons past Sechelt's long sunny beach of Davis Bay, Pender Harbour and Ruby Lake, passing by numerous coves and parks along its route.

Right: Paddlers train year-round for the annual Outrigger canoe races in July.

Below right: Sailors enjoy the scenic beauty of Howe Sound and the Coast Mountains.

Below: Howe Sound is a popular boating destination. A rainbow over Keats Island chases away clouds after a sudden shower.

Gibsons is a popular destination for boaters who come on week-end jaunts from Vancouver for sailboat races or to relax and browse in the local shops. All year long, avid paddlers train to compete in the annual Howe Sound Outrigger Race in July, Canada's largest outrigger event, which attracts competitors from as far away as California, Hawaii and Hong Kong.

Serious hikers ride the local passenger ferries to nearby Keats and Gambier Islands, where they share the trails and old logging roads with plentiful deer, hike up to Gambier Lake to fish for rainbow trout, or walk across Keats Island to swim at Eastbourne Beach.

There are many horse-back riding, bicycling and hiking trails on the Sunshine Coast: to the top of Mount Elphinstone, behind the pulp mill at Rainy River, into the ski areas of the pristine Tetrahedron Heights and along the newly built Sechelt Inlet Trail.

Several summer camps for city children have been established over the years on the Sunshine Coast's extensive shoreline. The Salvation Army and YMCA organizations have camps on each side of the Langdale ferry terminal. About one third of Keats Island is the property of the Baptist church and camps on Gambier Island provide opportunities for swimming and boating in the warm waters of Howe Sound. The Boy Scouts, Girl Guides and other groups have recreational properties along the Strait of Georgia between Roberts Creek and Sechelt.

A "Hawaii of the North" mural, "moon" signage, painted fish and banner art brighten Gibsons' waterfront streets and businesses.

Below far right: The tourist information centre in Pioneer Park in springtime.

Gibsons, as the Gateway to the Sunshine Coast, is a delightful blend of the old seaside fishing village mixed with modern cappucino, ice cream and gelatto shops and restaurants. There are shopping malls, art galleries and charming gift and antique stores. There is a waterfront park and a seawalk to the marina and Armour's Beach. For a west coast experience visitors can walk the Inglis Trail along the Charman Creek ravine from the harbour to Gibsons Heights. To view the town, a short hike to the lookout on top of Soames Hill provides the added treat of tasty huckleberries, salmonberries and blackberries picked along the way.

An abundance of art galleries, live theatre and musicians add an artistic flair to Gibsons. A highlight is the annual Fibre Arts Festival in August, an impressive showcase for handmade quilts and crafts. Colorful street banners, a weekly artisan market, jazz concerts and live music in Winegarden Waterfront Park and along the gazebo promenade attract strolling crowds on long, warm summer evenings. A full moon rising above Keats Island casts a magical glow over Howe Sound, on the boats in the harbour, and touches the bronzed shoulders of George Gibson in the park. As dusk settles over the town, the sparkling colored lights of Molly's Reach bring the friendly message of greeting to visitors and all those who have found a home in this safe harbour — "Welcome Back."

Top: Winter snow on the Coast Mountain range glows in the setting sun.

Right: A sunrise over Keats Island is reflected in the waters of Howe Sound.

Gibsons has been home to Vene Parnell and her family since 1979. She is a freelance photographer and writer and her articles have been published in numerous newspapers and magazines. She wrote and produced "The Beachcombers" souvenir book in 1984. Vene's photographs have won prizes and are sold in local shops and galleries on the Sunshine Coast.

Published by Sunshine Coast Scenics
www.suncoastscenics.com

Cover, interior design and maps by Roger Handling
Printed in Canada by Hemlock Printers
ISBN 0-9735747-0-4

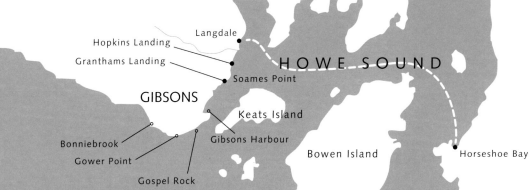

BRITISH COLUMBIA
Whistler
Squami
Powell River
SUNSHINE COAST
Comox
Pender Harbour
Sechelt
Gibsons
Horseshoe Bay
Vancouver
Nanaimo
Tsawwassen
VANCOUVER ISLAND
Swartz Bay
Pacific Ocean
Victoria
Juan de Fuca Strait

Port Mellon
Gambier Island
Roberts Creek
Langdale
Hopkins Landing
HOWE SOUND
Granthams Landing
Soames Point
GIBSONS
Keats Island
Bonniebrook
Gibsons Harbour
Gower Point
Bowen Island
Horseshoe Bay
Gospel Rock
STRAIT OF GEORGIA
VANCOUVER